BE

NOT

AFRAID

A BOOK OF QUOTES FOR CATHOLIC MEN

SAM GUZMAN

TABLE OF CONTENTS

The mouth of the righteous
utters wisdom, and his tongue
speaks justice.

PSALM 37:30

INTRODUCTION

One fine day, my mother handed me a book of quotes. It wasn't just any book of quotes—it was a collection of the wisdom of the Catholic saints. Neither of us was Catholic, and how that book came into her possession or why she gave it to me, I am still not entirely sure.

I was a young college student who had just come off a rather rough period of rebellion and had only recently returned to the things of God. I was zealously Reformed theologically—a devotee of the writings of John Calvin and the Puritans. I had no use for "popery"—and yet, for some reason I was intrigued by this little book, filled with one liners from men and women with strange sounding names.

Very quickly, however, curiosity turned into outright fascination, for the words on those pages exuded a kind of peace and joy—a fragrance of holiness, if you will—that captured my heart. Keep in mind that at the time, I believed that Catholics were in grave error, and that if any of them made it to heaven, it was in spite of their Catholic beliefs, but certainly not because of them. And yet, I saw something in these men and women that could only be described as sanctity. It was love, it was light, it was truth. It was the peace of Jesus Christ. That book stayed with me for years, growing tattered and torn from frequent use, and it accompanied me on my journey into the Catholic and Apostolic Church. No doubt I will return to its pages for many years to come, for the beauty of holiness never grows old.

I wrote this book in the hope that you will be transformed by the sanctity and wisdom of the saints as I was and still am. Their words and counsels show us the way to true happiness in a world that promises so many counterfeits. May we follow these men faithfully, so that someday we may rejoice with them before the throne of our great God and Savior, Jesus Christ.

In the hearts of Jesus and Mary,
Sam Guzman

FAITH

I.

To one who has faith, no explanation is necessary. To one without faith, no explanation is possible.

ST. THOMAS AQUINAS

If you believe what you like in the gospels, and reject what you don't like, it is not the gospel you believe, but yourself.

ST. AUGUSTINE

What is faith but a carriage to heaven?

ST. AELRED OF RIEVAULX

Most High, glorious God, enlighten the darkness of my heart and give me true faith, certain hope, and perfect charity, sense and knowledge, Lord, that I may carry out Your holy and true command.

ST. FRANCIS OF ASSISI

O my God, I firmly believe that Thou art one God in Three Divine Persons, Father, Son and Holy Ghost. I believe that Thy Divine Son became Man, and died for our sins, and that He will come to judge the living and the dead. I believe these and all the truths which the Holy Catholic Church teaches, because Thou hast revealed them, Who canst neither deceive nor be deceived.

ACT OF FAITH

Take care, then, to be firmly grounded in the teachings of the Lord and his apostles so that you may prosper in all your doings both in body and in soul, in faith and in love, in the Son, and in the Father and in the Spirit, in the beginning and in the end, along with your most worthy bishop and his spiritual crown, your presbyters, and with the deacons, who are men of God.

ST. IGNATIUS OF ANTIOCH

Faith comes to intelligence as a light that overflows it with joy and inspires it with a certitude that does away with question.

ETIENNE GILSON

But what we suffer from to-day is humility in the wrong place. Modesty has moved from the organ of ambition. Modesty has settled upon the organ of conviction; where it was never meant to be. A man was meant to be doubtful about himself, but undoubting about the truth; this has been exactly reversed.

G. K. CHESTERTON

It is idle to talk always of the alternative of reason and faith. Reason is itself a matter of faith. It is an act of faith to assert that our thoughts have any relation to reality at all.

G. K. CHESTERTON

You can't help feeling the fascination of a soul that knows what it wants, and lives by faith.

POPE ST. JOHN XXIII

Understanding is the reward of faith. Therefore, don't seek to understand so that you may believe, but believe so that you may understand.

ST. AUGUSTINE

The faith of those who live their faith is a serene faith. What you long for will be given you; what you love will be yours forever.

POPE ST. LEO THE GREAT

It is not the actual physical exertion that counts toward a man's progress, nor the nature of the task, but the spirit of faith with which it is undertaken.

ST. FRANCIS XAVIER

Every morning you put on your clothes to cover your nakedness and protect your body from inclement weather. Why don't you also clothe your soul with the garment of faith? Remember each morning the truths of your creed, and look at yourself in the mirror of your faith. Otherwise, your soul will soon be naked with the nakedness of oblivion.

ST. AUGUSTINE

The most beautiful act of faith is the one made in darkness, in sacrificing, and with extreme effort.

ST. PADRE PIO

Faith means believing the unbelievable, or it is no virtue at all.

G.K. CHESTERTON

Put into practice the teachings of our holy faith, it is not enough to convince ourselves that they are true; we must love them. Love united to faith makes us practice our religion.

ST. ALPHONSUS LIGUORI

God is always almighty; He can at all times work miracles, and He would work them now as in the days of old were it not that faith is lacking!

ST. JOHN VIANNEY

We must neither doubt nor hesitate with respect to the words of the Lord; rather, we must be fully persuaded that every word of God is true and possible, even if our nature should rebel against the idea; for in this lies the test of faith.

ST. BASIL THE GREAT

Faith furnishes prayer with wings, without which it cannot soar to heaven.

ST. JOHN CLIMACUS

O Catholic faith, how solid, how strong you are! How deeply rooted, how firmly founded on a solid rock! Heaven and earth will pass away, but you can never pass away.

From the beginning the world opposed you, but you mightily triumphed over everything. This is the victory that overcomes the world, our faith.

It has subjected powerful kings to the rule of Christ; it has bound nations to his service. What made the holy apostles and martyrs endure fierce agony and bitter torments, except faith, and especially faith in the resurrection?

What is it that today makes true followers of

Christ cast luxuries aside, leave pleasures behind, and endure difficulties and pain? It is living faith that expresses itself through love.

ST. FIDELIS OF SIGMARINGEN

LIFE

II.

Wherever the Catholic sun doth shine,
There's always laughter and good red wine.
At least I've always found it so.
Benedicamus Domino!

HILAIRE BELLOC

The Catholic Church is like a thick steak, a glass
of red wine, and a good cigar.

G.K. CHESTERTON

Be who you are, and be that well.

ST. FRANCIS DE SALES

Enjoy yourselves as much as you like, if only you keep from sin.

ST. JOHN BOSCO

In Catholicism, the pint, the pipe and the Cross can all fit together.

G.K. CHESTERTON

Men are like wine – some turn to vinegar, but the best improve with age.

POPE ST. JOHN XXIII

When it comes to life, the critical thing is whether you take things for granted or take things with gratitude.

G.K. CHESTERTON

Life with Christ is a wonderful adventure.

POPE ST. JOHN PAUL II

Laugh and grow strong.

ST. IGNATIUS LOYOLA

Break the conventions. Keep the commandments.

G.K. CHESTERTON

We should thank God for beer and burgundy by not drinking too much of them.

G.K. CHESTERTON

It is not always in your power to do important things; sufficient are the small things that offer themselves every hour of every day. So do them with devotion and love.

ST. FRANCIS DE SALES

If more of us valued food and cheer and song above hoarded gold, it would be a merrier world.

J.R. R. TOLKIEN

So abandon yourself utterly for the love of God, and in this way, you will become truly happy.

BL. HENRY SUSO

It is not our part to master all the tides of the world, but to do what is in us for the succor of those years wherein we are set, uprooting the evil in the fields that we know, so that those who live after may have clean earth to till. What weather they shall have is not ours to rule.

J.R.R. TOLKIEN

The needs of the times will teach you what to do.

BL. ADOLPH KOLPING

With Christians, a poetical view of things is a duty. We are bid to color all things with hues of faith, to see a divine meaning in every event.

BL. JOHN HENRY NEWMAN

God has created me to do him some definite service; he has committed some work to me which he has not committed to another. I have my mission - I may never know it in this life, but I shall be told it in the next...

BL. JOHN HENRY NEWMAN

True virtue is not sad or disagreeable, but pleasantly cheerful.

ST. JOSEMARIA ESCRIVA

Lord, make me an instrument of your peace; where there is hatred, let me sow love; where there is injury, pardon; where there is doubt, faith; where there is despair, hope; where there is darkness, light; and where there is sadness, joy.

ST. FRANCIS OF ASSISI

Christ be with me, Christ within me, Christ behind me, Christ before me, Christ beside me, Christ to win me, Christ to comfort me and restore me, Christ beneath me, Christ above me, Christ in quiet, Christ in danger, Christ in hearts of all that love me, Christ in mouth of friend and stranger.

ST. PATRICK

In eating, in drinking, in all that you do, do everything as for God's glory.

ST. PAUL

Let us desire nothing else, let us want nothing else, let nothing else please us and cause us delight except our Creator, Redeemer and Savior, the only true God, Who is the fullness of good, all good, every good, the true and supreme good, Who alone is good, merciful, gentle, delightful, and sweet, Who alone is holy, just, true, holy, and upright,

Who alone is kind, innocent, clean, from Whom, through Whom and in Whom is all pardon, all grace, all glory of all penitents and just ones, of all the blessed rejoicing together in heaven.

Wherever we are, in every place, at every hour, at every time of the day, every day and continually, let all of us truly and humbly believe, hold in our heart and love, honor, adore, serve, praise and bless, glorify and exalt, magnify and give thanks to the Most High and Supreme Eternal God, Trinity and Unity, Father, Son and Holy Spirit, Creator of all, Savior of all Who believe and hope in Him, and love Him, Who, without beginning and end, is unchangeable, invisible, indescribable, ineffable, incomprehensible, unfathomable, blessed, praiseworthy, glorious, exalted, sublime, most high, gentle, lovable, delightful, and totally desirable above all else forever.

ST. FRANCIS OF ASSISI

WORK

III.

Persevere in the exact fulfillment of the obligations of the moment. That work — humble, monotonous, small — is prayer expressed in action that prepares you to receive the grace of the other work — great and wide and deep — of which you dream.

ST. JOSEMARIA ESCRIVA

Pray and work.

ST. BENEDICT

Serve the Lord with Laughter.

ST. PADRE PIO

Great occasions for serving God come seldom, but little ones surround us daily.

ST. FRANCIS DE SALES

Think of what you are doing. Do not be concerned about anything else, whether bad or good.

ST. MAXIMILIAN KOLBE

How easily we could win heaven day by day just by doing what we have to do – but doing it for God!

ST. JOHN VIANNEY

Why are you in such a hurry? Go about your work slowly and peacefully, doing one thing at a time. You will make good progress.

ST. FRANCIS DE SALES

I am not capable of doing big things, but I want to do everything, even the smallest things, for the greater glory of God.

ST. DOMINIC SAVIO

Here is a rule for everyday life: Do not do anything which you cannot offer to God.

ST. JOHN VIANNEY

We cannot get to heaven on a feather bed.

ST. THOMAS MORE

Without work, it is impossible to have fun.

ST. THOMAS AQUINAS

Be great in little things.

ST. FRANCIS XAVIER

He who labors as he prays lifts his heart to God with his hands.

ST. BENEDICT

Your greatest enemy is idleness. Fight it without let up.

ST. JOHN BOSCO

Preserve order and order will preserve you.

ST. MAXIMILIAN KOLBE

Work, but only do as much as your strength can take.

ST. JOHN BOSCO

Pray as though everything depended on God. Work as though everything depended on you.

ST. AUGUSTINE

All of us can attain to Christian virtue and holiness, no matter in what condition of life we live and no matter what our life work may be.

ST. FRANCIS DE SALES

You must be careful: don't let your professional success or failure — which will certainly come — make you forget, even for a moment, what the true aim of your work is: the glory of God!

ST. JOSEMARIA ESCRIVA

Sanctifying one's work is no fantastic dream, but the mission of every Christian — yours and mine. That is what that lathe-worker had discovered, when he said: "I am overwhelmed with happiness when I think how true it is that while I am working at the lathe and singing — singing all the time, on the outside and on the inside — I can become a saint. How good God is!"

ST. JOSEMARIA ESCRIVA

Let us work. Let us work a lot and work well, without forgetting that prayer is our best weapon. That is why I will never tire of repeating that we have to be contemplative souls in the midst of the world, who try to convert their work into prayer.

ST. JOSEMARIA ESCRIVA

ASCETICISM

IV.

Fasting is the soul of prayer, mercy is the lifeblood of fasting. So if you pray, fast; if you fast, show mercy; if you want your petition to be heard, hear the petition of others.

ST. PETER CHRYSOLOGUS

We must fast with our whole heart, that is to say, willingly, whole-heartedly, universally and entirely.

ST. FRANCIS DE SALES

Without mortification, nothing can be done.

ST. PHILIP NERI

This exercise of bodily mortification—far removed from any form of stoicism—does not imply a condemnation of the flesh which sons of God deign to assume. On the contrary mortification aims at the "liberation" of man, who often finds himself, because of concupiscence, almost chained by his own senses. Through "corporal fasting" man regains strength and the "wound inflicted on the dignity of our nature by intemperance is cured by the medicine of a salutary abstinence."

BL. POPE PAUL VI

If you live according to the flesh, you shall die: but if by the Spirit you mortify the deeds of the flesh, you shall live.

ST. PAUL

Let us read the lives of the saints; let us consider the penances which they performed, and blush to be so effeminate and so fearful of mortifying our flesh.

ST. ALPHONSUS LIGUORI

The more one mortifies his natural inclinations, the more he renders himself capable of receiving divine inspirations and of progressing in virtue.

ST. FRANCIS DE SALES

Oh, how I like those little mortifications that are seen by nobody, such as rising a quarter of an hour sooner, rising for a little while in the night to pray!

ST. JOHN VIANNEY

Those who belong to Christ have crucified nature, with all its passions, all its impulses.

ST. PAUL

Let us fast an acceptable and very pleasing fast to the Lord. The true fast is the estrangement from evil, temperance of tongue, abstinence from anger, separation from desires, slander, falsehood and perjury. Privation of these is true fasting.

ST. BASIL THE GREAT

Be on your guard when you begin to mortify your body by abstinence and fasting, lest you imagine yourself to be perfect and a saint; for perfection does not consist in this virtue. It is only a help; a disposition; a means though a fitting one, for the attainment of true perfection.

ST. JEROME

If you are able to fast, you will do well to observe some days beyond what are ordered by the Church, for besides the ordinary effect of fasting in raising the mind, subduing the flesh, confirming goodness, and obtaining a heavenly reward, it is also a great matter to be able to control greediness, and to keep the sensual appetites and the whole body subject to the law of the Spirit; and although we may be able to do but little, the enemy nevertheless stands more in awe of those whom he knows can fast.

ST. FRANCIS DE SALES

Fasting gives birth to prophets and strengthens the powerful; fasting makes lawgivers wise. Fasting is a good safeguard for the soul, a steadfast companion for the body, a weapon for the valiant, and a gymnasium for athletes. Fasting repels temptations, anoints unto piety; it is the comrade of watchfulness and the artificer of chastity. In war it fights bravely, in peace it teaches stillness.

ST. BASIL THE GREAT

Renounce yourself in order to follow Christ; discipline your body; do not pamper yourself, but love fasting.

ST. BENEDICT

Asceticism and mortification are not the ends of a Christian life; they are only the means. The end is charity. Penance merely makes an opening in our ego in which the Light of God can pour. As we deflate ourselves, God fills us. And it is God's arrival that is the important event.

VEN. FULTON J. SHEEN

Doing penance for one's sins is a first step towards obtaining forgiveness and winning eternal salvation. That is the clear and explicit teaching of Christ, and no one can fail to see how justified and how right the Catholic Church has always been in constantly insisting on this. No individual Christian can grow in perfection, nor can Christianity gain in vigor, except it be on the basis of penance.

POPE ST. JOHN XXIII

Never forget that there are only two philosophies to rule your life: the one of the cross, which starts with the fast and ends with the feast. The other of Satan, which starts with the feast and ends with the headache.

VEN. FULTON J. SHEEN

No one whose stomach is full can fight mentally against the demon of unchastity. Our initial struggle therefore must be to gain control of our stomach and to bring our body into subjection not only through fasting but also through vigils, labors and spiritual reading, and through concentrating our heart on fear of Hell and on longing for the kingdom of heaven.

ST. JOHN CASSIAN

It seems abundantly clear that fasting represents an important ascetical practice, a spiritual arm to do battle against every possible disordered attachment to ourselves. Freely chosen detachment from the pleasure of food and other material goods helps the disciple of Christ to control the appetites of nature, weakened by original sin, whose negative effects impact the entire human person. Since all of us are weighed down by sin and its consequences, fasting is proposed to us as an instrument to restore friendship with God.

POPE BENEDICT XVI

PRAYER

V.

It is simply impossible to lead, without the aid of prayer, a virtuous life.

ST. JOHN CHRYSOSTOM

Virtues are formed by prayer. Prayer preserves temperance. Prayer suppresses anger. Prayer prevents emotions of pride and envy. Prayer draws into the soul the Holy Spirit, and raises man to heaven.

ST. EPHRAEM OF SYRIA

Pray without ceasing.

ST. PAUL

Prayer is the place of refuge for every worry, a foundation for cheerfulness, a source of constant happiness, a protection against sadness.

ST. JOHN CHRYSOSTOM

We must speak to God as a friend speaks to his friend, servant to his master; now asking some favor, now acknowledging our faults, and communicating to Him all that concerns us, our thoughts, our fears, our projects, our desires, and in all things seeking His counsel.

ST. IGNATIUS OF LOYOLA

When we pray, the voice of the heart must be heard more than proceedings from the mouth.

ST. BONAVENTURE

As our body cannot live without nourishment, so our soul cannot spiritually be kept alive without prayer.

ST. AUGUSTINE

It is true that God's power triumphs over everything, but humble and suffering prayer prevails over God Himself.

ST. PADRE PIO

It is better to say one Our Father fervently and devoutly than a thousand with no devotion and full of distraction.

ST. EDMUND

Without prayer nothing good is done. God's works are done with our hands joined, and on our knees. Even when we run, we must remain spiritually kneeling before Him.

BL. LUIGI ORIONE

Prayer ought to be short and pure, unless it be prolonged by the inspiration of Divine grace.

ST. BENEDICT

You don't know how to pray? Put yourself in the presence of God, and as soon as you have said, 'Lord, I don't know how to pray!' you can be sure you have already begun.

ST. JOSEMARIA ESCRIVA

Have confidence in prayer. It is the unfailing power which God has given us. By means of it you will obtain the salvation of the dear souls whom God has given you and all your loved ones. "Ask and you shall receive," Our Lord said. Be yourself with the good Lord.

ST. PETER JULIAN EYMARD

Prayer is nothing else than union with God. When the heart is pure and united with God it is consoled and filled with sweetness; it is dazzled by a marvelous light.

ST. JOHN VIANNEY

He who prays most receives most.

ST. ALPHONSUS LIGUORI

There is nothing more powerful than a person praying well.

ST. JOHN CHRYSOSTOM

Do nothing at all unless you begin with prayer.

ST. EPHRAEM THE SYRIAN

Prayer gives us strength for great ideals, for keeping up our faith, charity, purity, generosity; prayer gives us strength to rise up from indifference and guilt, if we have had the misfortune to give in to temptation and weakness. Prayer gives us light by which to see and to judge from God's perspective and from eternity. That is why you must not give up on praying!

POPE ST. JOHN PAUL II

You must speak to Jesus also with the heart, besides with the lips; indeed, in certain cases you must speak to Him only with the heart.

ST. PADRE PIO

Fasting detaches you from this world. Prayer reattaches you to the next world.

VEN. FULTON J. SHEEN

Every one of us needs half an hour of prayer a day, except when we are busy—then we need an hour.

ST. FRANCIS DE SALES

Pray with great confidence, with confidence based on the goodness and infinite generosity of God and upon the promises of Jesus Christ. God is a spring of living water which flows unceasingly into the hearts of those who pray.

ST. LOUIS DE MONTFORT

In a world where there is so much noise, so much bewilderment, there is a need for silent adoration of Jesus concealed in the Host. Be assiduous in the prayer of adoration and teach it to the faithful. It is a source of comfort and light, particularly to those who are suffering.

POPE BENEDICT XVI

Blessed is he who prays with fervor, for the devil never approaches him.

ST. EPHRAEM THE SYRIAN

Prayer is the foundation of the spiritual edifice. Prayer is all powerful.

ST. JOSEMARIA ESCRIVA

Faith and prayer. These are our weapons and our supports.

ST. JOHN BOSCO

Pray! Pray, but with faith – with living faith! Courage! Onward, ever onward!

ST. JOHN BOSCO

TRIALS

VI.

Whenever anything disagreeable or displeasing happens to you, remember Christ crucified and be silent.

ST. JOHN OF THE CROSS

Let us understand that God is a physician, and that suffering is a medicine for salvation, not a punishment for damnation.

ST. AUGUSTINE

The more we are afflicted in this world, the greater is our assurance in the next; the more we sorrow in the present, the greater will be our joy in the future.

ST. ISIDORE OF SEVILLE

All the darkness in the world cannot extinguish the light of a single candle.

ST. FRANCIS OF ASSISI

A thousand difficulties do not make a single doubt.

BL. JOHN HENRY CARDINAL NEWMAN

Trials and tribulations offer us a chance to make reparation for our past faults and sins. On such occasions the Lord comes to us like a physician to heal the wounds left by our sins. Tribulation is the divine medicine.

ST. AUGUSTINE

If you embrace all things in this life as coming from the hands of God, and even embrace death to fulfill His holy will, assuredly you will die a saint.

ST. ALPHONSUS LIGUORI

Would that men might come at last to see that it is quite impossible to reach the thicket of the riches and wisdom of God except by first entering the thicket of much suffering, in such a way that the soul finds there its consolation and desire. The soul that longs for divine wisdom chooses first, and in truth, to enter the thicket of the cross.

ST. JOHN OF THE CROSS

Jesus who cannot suffer long to keep you in affliction will come to relieve and comfort you by infusing fresh courage into your soul.

ST. PADRE PIO

Let us not esteem worldly prosperity or adversity as things real or of any moment, but let us live elsewhere, and raise all our attention to heaven; esteeming sin as the only true evil, and nothing truly good, but virtue which unites us to God.

ST. GREGORY NAZIANZEN

Each man, in his suffering, can also become a sharer in the redemptive suffering of Christ.

POPE ST. JOHN PAUL II

Trials, tests and battles are meant to strengthen us, not weaken us.

ST. CYPRIAN

God created shadows to better emphasize the light.

POPE ST. JOHN XXIII

It is necessary to be strong, in order to become great; that is our duty. Life is a struggle, which we cannot avoid. We must triumph!

ST. PADRE PIO

Jesus promised his disciples three things—that they would be completely fearless, absurdly happy, and in constant trouble.

G.K. CHESTERTON

The Lord sometimes makes you feel the weight of the cross. Although the weight seems intolerable, you are able to carry it, because the Lord, in His love and mercy extends a hand to you and gives you strength.

ST. PADRE PIO

Our pilgrimage on earth cannot be exempt from trial. We progress by means of trial. No one knows himself except through trial, or receive a crown except after a victory, or strives except against an enemy or temptations.

ST. AUGUSTINE

You must either suffer in this life or give up the hope of seeing God in heaven. Sufferings and persecutions are of the greatest avail to us, because we can find therein a very efficient means to make atonement for our sins, since we are bound to suffer for them either in this world or in the next.

ST. JOHN VIANNEY

The Cross is the way to Paradise, but only when it is borne willingly.

ST. PAUL OF THE CROSS

The cross is the greatest gift God could bestow on His Elect on earth. There is nothing so necessary, so beneficial, so sweet, or so glorious as to suffer something for Jesus. If you suffer as you ought, the cross will become a precious yoke that Jesus will carry with you.

ST. LOUIS DE MONTFORT

Let us tell ourselves that every day, every hour, every instant of suffering borne with Jesus and for love of Him will be a new heaven for all eternity, and a new glory given God for ever.

BL. COLUMBA MARMION

HUMILITY

VII.

No man can attain to the knowledge of God but by humility. The way to mount high is to descend.

BL. GILES OF ASSISI

Be humble in this life that God may raise you up in the next.

ST. STEPHEN OF HUNGARY

The most powerful weapon to conquer the devil is humility. For, as he does not know at all how to employ it, neither does he know how to defend himself from it.

ST. VINCENT DE PAUL

No one reaches the kingdom of heaven except by humility.

ST. AUGUSTINE

Humility, which is a virtue, is always fruitful in good works.

ST. THOMAS AQUINAS

The highest point of humility consists in not merely acknowledging one's abjection, but in taking pleasure therein, not from any want of breadth or courage, but to give the more glory to God's Divine Majesty, and to esteem one's neighbor more highly than one's self.

ST. FRANCIS DE SALES

Humility is the mother of many virtues because from it obedience, fear, reverence, patience, modesty, meekness and peace are born. He who is humble easily obeys everyone, fears to offend anyone, is at peace with everyone, is kind with all.

ST. THOMAS OF VILLANOVA

There is something in humility which strangely exalts the heart.

ST. AUGUSTINE

I wish I could lose myself and never find myself except in God!

ST. JOHN VIANNEY

Do you wish to rise? Begin by descending. You plan a tower that will pierce the clouds? Lay first the foundation of humility.

ST. AUGUSTINE

Clothe yourselves, all of you, with humility toward one another, for "God opposes the proud, but gives grace to the humble."

ST. PETER

God takes especial delight in the humility of a man who believes that he has not yet begun to do any good.

ST. PHILIP NERI

If pride made demons out of angels, there is no doubt that humility could make angels out of demons.

ST. JOHN CLIMACUS

In the order of the virtues, humility holds the first rank. In this sense, that it drives from us pride, which sets us at war with God, and that, on the contrary, it renders man submissive and entirely open to the effusions of Divine grace.

ST. THOMAS AQUINAS

By humility a man finds grace before God and peace with men.

BL. GILES OF ASSISI

A good Christian should be humble as was Jesus Christ, Who knelt down to wash the feet of His apostles. He washed even Judas' feet, although He knew that the traitor was going to betray Him. The true Christian should consider himself to be the least among others and the servant of all.

ST. JOHN BOSCO

Be humble in order to be joyful, because joy goes hand in hand with humility.

ST. PACHOMIUS

The truly humble reject all praise for themselves, and refer it all to God.

ST. ALPHONSUS LIGUORI

Don't wish to be like the gilded weather-cock on top of a great building: however much it shines, and however high it stands, it adds nothing to the solidity of the building. Rather be like an old stone block hidden in the foundations, underground, where no one can see you: because of you the house will not fall.

ST. JOSEMARIA ESCRIVA

The first degree of humility is the fear of God, which we should constantly have before our eyes.

ST. LOUIS DE BLOIS

You must ask God to give you power to fight against the sin of pride which is your greatest enemy – the root of all that is evil, and the failure of all that is good. For God resists the proud.

ST. VINCENT DE PAUL

The thief who received the kingdom of heaven, though not as the reward of virtue, is a true witness to the fact that salvation is ours through the grace and mercy of God. All of our holy fathers knew this and all with one accord teach that perfection in holiness can be achieved only through humility. Humility, in its turn, can be achieved only through faith, fear of God, gentleness and the shedding of all possessions. It is by means of these that we attain perfect love, through the grace and compassion of our Lord Jesus Christ, to whom be glory through all the ages. Amen.

ST. JOHN CASSIAN

COURAGE

VIII.

The world offers you comfort, but you were not made for comfort. You were made for greatness.

POPE BENEDICT XVI

Be a man. Don't blush for your convictions.

ST. MAXIMILIAN KOLBE

Courage! God asks of us only our good will. His grace does the rest.

ST. THEOPHANE VENARD

One of the things we absolutely owe our Lord is to never be afraid.

BL. CHARLES DE FOUCAULD

There is only one thing to be feared and that is sin. Everything else is beside the point.

ST. JOHN CHRYSOSTOM

Do not be afraid. Do not be satisfied with mediocrity. Put out into the deep and let down your nets for a catch.

POPE ST. JOHN PAUL II

I plead with you—never, ever give up on hope, never doubt, never tire, and never become discouraged. Be not afraid.

POPE ST. JOHN PAUL II

When God is with us, we do not need to be afraid.

BL. PIER GIORGIO FRASSATI

Remember that you will derive strength by reflecting that the saints yearn for you to join their ranks; desire to see you fight bravely, and that you behave like true knights in your encounters with the same adversities which they had to conquer, and that breathtaking joy is theirs and your eternal reward for having endured a few years of temporal pain. Every drop of earthly bitterness will be changed into an ocean of heavenly sweetness.

BL. HENRY SUSO

We shall steer safely through every storm, so long as our heart is right, our intention fervent, our courage steadfast, and our trust fixed on God.

ST. FRANCIS DE SALES

You can do more with the grace of God than you think.

ST. JOHN BAPTISTE DE LA SALLE

Do not blush to be a servant of Christ.

ST. PAUL OF THE CROSS

You must accept your cross: If you bear it courageously, it will carry you to heaven.

ST. JOHN VIANNEY

Have faith. Everything will be all right. Faith, faith!

ST. LEOPOLD MADIC

I do not care very much what men say of me, provided that God approves of me.

ST. THOMAS MORE

In our time more than ever before, the chief strength of the wicked lies in the cowardice and weakness of good men.

POPE ST. PIUS X

My hope is in Christ, who strengthens the weakest by His divine help; I can do all in Him who strengthened me! His power is infinite, and if I lean on Him it will be mine; His wisdom is infinite, and if I look to Him for counsel I shall not be deceived; His goodness is infinite, and if my trust is stayed on Him I shall not be abandoned. Hope unites me to my God and Him to me. Although I know I am not sufficient for the burden, my strength is in Him. For the salvation of others I must bear weariness, face dangers, suffer offenses, confront storms, fight against evil. He is my Hope.

POPE ST. PIUS X

I see Mary everywhere. I see difficulties nowhere.

ST. MAXIMILIAN KOLBE

Courage is almost a contradiction in terms. It means a strong desire to live taking the form of a readiness to die.

G.K. CHESTERTON

Virtue demands courage, constant effort, and above all, help from on high.

ST. JOHN VIANNEY

Let those very obstacles give you strength. God's grace will not fail you: *Inter medium montium pertransibunt aquae!* You shall pass through the mountains!

ST. JOSEMARIA ESCRIVA

We're on the Lord's team, therefore we are on the winning side. Let us raise our glasses.

POPE BENEDICT XVI

PURITY

IX.

Holy Purity is granted by God when it is asked for with humility.

ST. JOSEMARIA ESCRIVA

Chastity is a difficult, long term matter; one must wait patiently for it to bear fruit, for the happiness of loving kindness which it must bring. But at the same time, chastity is the sure way to happiness.

POPE ST. JOHN PAUL II

In temptations against chastity, the spiritual masters advise us, not so much to contend with the bad thought, as to turn the mind to some spiritual, or, at least, indifferent object. It is useful to combat other bad thoughts face to face, but not thoughts of impurity.

ST. ALPHONSUS LIGUORI

God has assigned as a duty to every man the dignity of every woman.

POPE ST. JOHN PAUL II

Holy Purity, the queen of virtues, the angelic virtue, is a jewel so precious that those who possess it become like the angels of God in heaven, even though clothed in mortal flesh.

ST. JOHN BOSCO

Purity prepares the soul for love, and love confirms the soul in purity.

BL. JOHN HENRY NEWMAN

Chastity is the lily of virtues, and makes men almost equal to angels. Everything is beautiful in accordance with its purity. Now the purity of man is chastity, which is called honesty, and the observance of it, honor and also integrity; and its contrary is called corruption; in short, it has this peculiar excellence above the other virtues, that it preserves both soul and body fair and unspotted.

ST. FRANCIS DE SALES

There is no remedy as powerful against the heat of concupiscence as the remembrance of our Savior's Passion. In all my difficulties I never found anything so efficacious as the wounds of Christ: In them I sleep secure; from them I derive new life.

ST. AUGUSTINE

Humility is the safeguard of chastity. In the matter of purity, there is no greater danger than not fearing the danger. For my part, when I find a man secure of himself and without fear, I give him up for lost. I am less alarmed for one who is tempted and who resists by avoiding the occasions, than for one who is not tempted and is not careful to avoid occasions. When a person puts himself in an occasion, saying, I shall not fall, it is an almost infallible sign that he will fall, and with great injury to his soul.

ST. PHILIP NERI

There is need for a crusade of manliness and purity to counteract and nullify the savage work of those who think man is a beast. And that crusade is your work.

ST. JOSEMARIA ESCRIVA

It is well known, and is daily experienced by the clients of Mary, that her powerful name gives the particular strength necessary to overcome temptations against purity.

ST. ALPHONSUS LIGUORI

Devotion to the Blessed Sacrament and devotion to the Blessed Mother are not simply the best way, but in fact the only way to keep purity. At the age of 20, nothing but communion can keep one's heart pure. Chastity is not possible without the Eucharist.

ST. PHILIP NERI

As the pilot of a vessel is tried in the storm, as the wrestler is tried in the ring, the soldier in battle, and the hero in adversity, so is the Christian tried in temptation.

ST. BASIL THE GREAT

To defend his purity St. Francis of Assisi rolled in the snow, St. Benedict threw himself into a thorn bush, St. Bernard plunged himself into an icy pond. You, what have you done? Don't say that's the way I am, it's my character.

No! It's your lack of character.

Be a man! When you decide firmly to live a pure life, chastity will not be a burden on you, it will be a crown of triumph.

ST. JOSEMARIA ESCRIVA

Earthly continence is a sign that the body, whose end is not the grave, is directed to glorification. Already by this very fact, continence for the kingdom of heaven, is a witness among men that anticipates the future resurrection.

POPE ST. JOHN PAUL II

In order to acquire this perfect mastery of the spirit over the senses, it is not enough to refrain from acts directly contrary to chastity, but it is necessary also generously to renounce anything that may offend this virtue nearly or remotely; at such a price will the soul be able to reign fully over the body and lead its spiritual life in peace and liberty.

POPE PIUS XII

LOVE

X.

We are to love God for Himself, because of a twofold reason; nothing is more reasonable, nothing more profitable.

ST. BERNARD OF CLAIRVAUX

Give something, however small, to the one in need. For it is not small to one who has nothing. Neither is it small to God, if we have given what we could.

ST. GREGORY NAZIANZEN

God is Love. We eventually have to ask ourselves the question; why was Love nailed to a cross?

POPE ST. JOHN PAUL II

Charity is that with which no man is lost, and without which no man is saved.

ST. ROBERT BELLARMINE

Love is the most necessary of all virtues. Love in the person who preaches the word of God is like fire in a musket. If a person were to throw a bullet with his hands, he would hardly make a dent in anything; but if the person takes the same bullet and ignites some gunpowder behind it, it can kill. It is much the same with the word of God. If it is spoken by someone who is filled with the fire of charity—the fire of love of God and neighbor—it will work wonders.

ST. ANTHONY MARY CLARET

You learn to speak by speaking, to study by studying, to run by running, to work by working, and just so, you learn to love by loving. All those who think to learn in any other way deceive themselves.

ST. FRANCIS DE SALES

The proof of love is in the works. Where love exists, it works great things. But when it ceases to act, it ceases to exist.

POPE ST. GREGORY THE GREAT

The things that we love tell us what we are.

ST. THOMAS AQUINAS

What does love look like? It has the hands to help others. It has the feet to hasten to the poor and needy. It has eyes to see misery and want. It has the ears to hear the sighs and sorrows of men. That is what love looks like.

ST. AUGUSTINE

We must love our neighbor as being made in the image of God and as an object of His love.

ST. VINCENT DE PAUL

Eucharist is the Sacrament of love; it signifies love, it produces love. The Eucharist is the consummation of the whole spiritual life.

ST. THOMAS AQUINAS

The person who loves God cannot help loving every man as himself, even though he is grieved by the passions of those who are not yet purified. But when they amend their lives, his delight is indescribable and knows no bounds. A soul filled with thoughts of sensual desire and hatred is unpurified. If we detect any trace of hatred in our hearts against any man whatsoever for committing any fault, we are utterly estranged from love for God, since love for God absolutely precludes us from hating any man.

ST. MAXIMOS THE CONFESSOR

There is no place for selfishness—and no place for fear! Do not be afraid, then, when love makes demands. Do not be afraid when love requires sacrifice.

POPE ST. JOHN PAUL II

Real love is demanding. I would fail in my mission if I did not tell you so. Love demands a personal commitment to the will of God.

POPE ST. JOHN PAUL II

Since love grows within you, so beauty grows. For love is the beauty of the soul.

ST. AUGUSTINE

God loves each of us as if there were only one of us.

ST. AUGUSTINE

He alone loves the Creator perfectly who manifests a pure love for his neighbor.

ST. BEDE

Charity may be a very short word, but with its tremendous meaning of pure love, it sums up man's entire relation to God and to his neighbor.

ST. AELRED OF RIEVAULX

Charity unites us to God... There is nothing mean in charity, nothing arrogant. Charity knows no schism, does not rebel, does all things in concord. In charity all the elect of God have been made perfect.

POPE ST. CLEMENT I

It is by the path of love, which is charity, that God draws near to man, and man to God. But where charity is not found, God cannot dwell. If, then, we possess charity, we possess God, for "God is Charity."

ST. ALBERT THE GREAT

Nothing is sweeter than love, nothing stronger or higher or wider; nothing is more pleasant, nothing fuller, and nothing better in heaven or on earth, for love is born of God and cannot rest except in God, Who is above all created things. Love is watchful. Sleeping, it does not slumber. Wearied, it is not tired. Pressed, it is not straitened. Alarmed, it is not confused, but like a living flame, a burning torch, it forces its way upward and passes unharmed through every obstacle.

THOMAS A KEMPIS

Love means loving that which is unlovable, or it means nothing at all.

G.K. CHESTERTON

Made in the USA
Columbia, SC
23 December 2019